The Little Book of Red Hair

z

The moral rights of author Martin Ellis has been asserted.

Cover artwork Paul Goldsmith

Cover design Nick Ridley

Printed & bound in Great Britain by
William Clowes Ltd, Beccles, Suffolk
ISBN 978 1903506 271
Published by Zymurgy Publishing,
Newcastle upon Tyne
10 9 8 7 6 5 4 3 2

In memory of Bryan, my father who relatives told me had red hair in his younger days and gave me my red hair. His ended his days with white hair.

Acknowledgments

Many thanks to the following; Charlie Allen, Natalie Carr, Kat Mattieson (hair on the front cover), Ross Mowbray, Randall Northam and Charlotte Rushton.

The Roots of Desire by Marion Roach

Redandproud.com

Wikipedia

In recent years medical research and the human genome project has provided scientific explanations for the science of red hair.

What Causes Red Hair?

As one would expect red hair is determined by genetics, the DNA passed on by our parents. To have red hair it is necessary for both parents to carry the melanocortin 1 receptor (MC1R), although they may not have red hair themselves.

Research is still ongoing and much more needs to be

learnt, the alleles Arg151Cys, Arg160Trp, Asp294His, and Arg142His on MC1R have been identified as recessives for the red hair phenotype. The gene are primarily found on chromosomes 15 and 19, It is also possible that red hair is influenced by gene HCL2 (aka RHC, RHA) on chromosome 4.

Who identified the cause of red hair?

In the early 1990s Roger Cone from Oregon recognised the significance of the MC1R as the gene effecting human pigmentation.

A few years later Jonathan L Rees, Professor of Dermatology at the University of Edinburgh with colleagues Tony Thody

(Newcastle) and Ian Jackson (Edinburgh) demonstrated that red heads have variants of this gene.

Will red hair become extinct?

It has been suggested that as red hair is caused by recessive genes it may die out in the next hundred years. Scientic opinion does not support this hypothesis.

What makes red hair red?

Skin and hair contains two sorts of pigment: eumelanin, which is brown or black, and pheomelanin, which is red or yellow. The combination of eumelanin and pheomelanin determines hair colour.

A key chemical in colorisation is trichosiderin, research into the importance of the chemical has found that only people with red hair have a high concentration of trichosiderin (however, some red heads do not).

Why are red heads so susceptile to sun burn?

A bit of a double whammy for red heads.

Firstly redheads have red melanosomes in their skin whilst dark haired people have black melanosmes. Red melanosomes are significantly more reactive than black melanosomes.

Secondly, redheads have less melanin which protects reflects and absorbs harmful UV rays.

Fair skin and red hair is genetically linked, redheads are significantly more at risk to skin cancer than people with darker skin.

Why do so many redheads have freckles?

Freckles are not an exclusive characteristic of red hair, however, they are a characteristic of fair skin. Fair skin has less melanin, but there can be small concentrations of pigment cells with extra melanin within the skin that tan easily producing freckles.

It is true that redheads have a greater pain threshold?

Generations of anaesthetists have anecdotally passed on advice that they need to increase the dose to anaesthetise redheads.

Academic research at Louisville University in Kentucky published in 2002 confirmed that people with red hair feel pain more easily than most and extra anaesthetic is required for red haired patients.

How does red hair age?

Red hair maintains its natural colour longer than other hair types. When red hair ages it does not go grey, but goes sandy–blond before eventually turning white.

Are than any differences in the composition of red hair on the scalp?

Red heads usually have less hair on their scalp. On average adult blonds have 140,000 hairs, brunettes have 110,000 and redheads have 90,000 hairs on their scalp.

Why do redheads rarely have brown eyes?

It is unlikely that the gene for brown eyes will be recognised on a chromosome carrying the gene for red hair. For someone to have red hair and brown eyes they would require two copies of the gene for red hair with at least one copy of the gene for brown hair.

Blue is the most common eye colour for red heads.

Are there any medical problems associated with red hair?

Brittle Cornea Syndrome is very rare and occurs occasionally in Tunisian Jews. People effected always have red hair as well as brittle corneas, a bluish shade to the the whites of the eyes, hyperextensible joints and hyeprelastic skin.

Can dark hair turn red?

Malnutrition can cause dark hair to turn red, due to protein deficiency. This is a characteristic of a syndrome called kwashiorkor which occurs in famines. It has also been observed with pack–backers who fail to ensure that they maintain a proper diet.

When did homo sapiens first have red hair?

Oxford University scientists think that the gene for red hair could well be 100,000 years old, they have identified it in Neanderthal man, who died out 28,000 years ago in Spain and southwest France.

Animals with red hair

* cats
* cattle
* deer
* dogs
* fox
* giraffes
* horses
* kite
* red–bellied lemur
* orangutan
* panda
* Rhode Island Red
* squirrel

Don't try to dye your hair!

Be proud of your red hair and don't try to change it. Red hair is difficult to dye and has a tendancy to turn green!

It is possible to dye or bleach red hair, but it is a difficult job that needs to done by a professional.

Who says red hair is unpopular?

Red is the most popular colour selected by women who choose to dye their hair. A report found that sixty per cent of women who dye their hair at home, dye their hair red.

Most pixies have red hair!

Ancient Egypt

It is believed that a number of pharoes and ancient Egyptians had red hair; Ramses II, Seqenenre (17th Dynasty), Thuya (18th Dynasty). It has been questioned whether the red hair has been created by the mummification process.

However there is clear evidence that Ramses II was a

red head. Cleopatra died her hair red with henna.

Whilst Cleopatra may have been passionate about red hair, her view was not shared by all in ancient Egypt, there are also reports of Egyptians burning redheads and burying them alive.

Lilith

The first wife of Adam had red hair. She is considered by many feminists to be the ultimate heroine.

Lilith features in the old testament and Hebrew writings.

Judas Iscariot

Judas Iscariot is often portrayed with red hair and a beard, his alleged characteristics have created a myth. There is nothing in the bible that describes the physical appearance of Judas. The image of Judas was created in northern Europe in the middle–ages and renaissance.

Romans and redheads

Red haired slaves were bought and sold for a premium by Romans'. This may be the roots of the mythology regarding the sexual powers, prowess and performance of red heads.

Emperor Nero was a red head, born in Corsica famous for playing his violin whilst

Rome burnt had a reputation for enjoying life; drinking, watching gladiators fight at the Coliseum and partying Roman style.

Witches and persecution of red heads

German folklore believed that redheads were witches. Between 1483–1784 thousands of suspected witches were stripped and searched for "marks of the devil", such as freckles, moles, warts, and birthmarks. Red hair was considered an abnormality and possibly people were scared of it. There are estimates that around 45,000 women were tortured and murdered, usually by burning at the stake or by drowning.

The medieval church was responsible for promoting persecution of red haired women across Europe in the middle-ages. During the Spanish Inquisition redheads were regularly burnt. Many red heads were also burnt in England, however this practice stopped when Elizabeth I became Queen of England.

Greek mythology

King Nisus of Megara had to keep a lock of red hair in his own white hair to ensure the protection of Megara. When King Minos attacked Megara, Scylla, who was the daughter of Nisus fell in love with King Minos. To prove her love she cut of a lock of hair from her father's head, which killed him. Subsequently Megara fell to

King Nisus when he discovered that Scylla was responsible for her father's death, King Nisus then killed Scylla.

There are a number of redheads in Greek mythology including;

Eos – a beautiful woman with white wings and flowing red hair.

Odysseus – featured in Homer's poem the Odyssey.

Medussa – a gruesome monster who became a Marvel comic character with powers and strength in his long, thick red hair.

There is a Greek myth that red heads turn into vampires when they die.

Mecca

Every year around two million Muslim pilgrims journey to Mecca, a tradition that dates back to the time of Ibrahim. The process takes nine days and is followed on the tenth day by the festival of the sacrifice, Eid al Adha. Returning pilgrims dye their hair red using henna.

Red hair and good luck

It is considered an honour to have a red haired baby in Denmark.

In Poland if you pass three red heads it will bring you good luck and you will win the lottery!

Many old ladies believe that stroking or rubbing the head of a child with red hair will bring good luck.

Most red haired children do not consider it lucky to be molested by old ladies.

Shades of red

* auburn
* chestnut
* cinnamon
* copper red
* flame red
* ginger
* golden red
* russet
* scarlet
* strawberry blond

The country name Russia means "land of redheads" in honour of red head viking Rurik.

British Monarchs

Britain has had a number of red haired monarchs, Prince Harry demonstrates that the red gene is still present in the Royal family, so it is possible that in the future there will be another red haired king or queen.

Boadica, Queen of the Iceni

A legendary celtic monarch with a reputation for striking fear into her enemy. She successfully battled against the Romans.

William the Conqueror

The last person to lead a successful invasion of England as everyone remembers in 1066.

William II

Known as William Rufus, the second surviving son of William the Conqueror. He was involved in military campaigns in Wales, Scotland and France. Whilst his father funded churches, William II did not suport the church, instead he raided monasteries for funds.

Henry II

Ruled for twenty-five years but spent thirteen years in what is now France. He was regarded as a strong leader.

Henry VIII

All school kids know him as the King with six wives who destroyed monasteries because the church would not grant him a divorce.

Mary Queen of Scots

Mary spent much of her life locked up in English castles, a lock of her red hair can be seen at Hollyrood House in Edinburgh.

Elizabeth I

Known as the Virgin Queen, she was the last of the Tudors.

The house of Tudors had three red head monarchs in succession.

Queen Victoria

Britain's longest serving monarch she had an era named after her. Victoria is often satirised by the statement "I am not amused", however she loved to sing, draw and paint. When her husband Albert died she spent forty years in mourning.

Other red Royals

Anne Boleyn the second wife of Henry VIII and mother of Elizabeth I.

King David the second King of Israel.

"Red is the colour of colour of power."

Marion Roach

Politicians

Red heads have been key players in the political history of Britain.

Paddy Ashdown

Leader of the Liberal Democrats, ex–Royal Marine and Special Boat Service member.

Herbert Asquith

Early 20th Century Liberal Prime Minister his nickname was "The Sledgehammer".

Barbara Castle

Passionate old school Labour M.P., as Minister for Transport she introduced the 70 mph speed limit, breathalyser and compulsory seat belts.

Sir Winston Churchill

Regarded by many as the greatest P.M. ever, he was the first Lord of the Admiralty following the outbreak of World War II and led Britain through the war. During his time in Parliament he crossed the house from Conservative to Liberal and back to the Conservative party.

Robin Cook

Labour M.P., Foreign Secretary and keen follower of the turf, gained respect for resigning from the cabinet over the Iraq war.

Charles Kennedy

Former leader of the Liberal Democrats, Red and Proud's Redhead of the Year 2003.

Neil Kinnock

Former Labour leader who has now lost most of his red hair. After leaving the commons he served as the U.K. Commissioner of the European Commission.

"Out of the ash

I rise with red

hair. And east

men like air."

Sylvia Plath

"Whilst the rest
of the species
is descendend
from apes,
red heads are
descended
from cats."

Mark Twain (also a redhead)

Art and Literature

Vincent van Gogh, Titian and Matisse were red heads. Many artists favoured red haired models; Dante Rossetti's Pandora is based on Jane Morris, Lizzie Siddle modelled for a number of pre–raphaelite artists. Bottichelli and Titian are famous for their portraits of redheads.

Fictional redheads

It is claimed that J.K. Rowling is fascinated by red hair and selected Stuart Pearson to paint her portrait for the National Portrait Gallery because she was impressed by his paintings of red heads. Most of the Weasley family in the Harry Potter stories have red hair including Harry's best friend Ron.

Many characters in children's books are redheads; Peter Pan, Anne of Greengables, Pippi Longstocking, Little Orphan Annie, William Brown's friend Ginger in Just William and aviator Biggles close mate Ginger.

A number of cartoon characters have red hair; Ariel the Little Mermaid (voted the most well known red head in an

American poll), Tin Tin, Gordon
Tracey from Thunderbirds and
Postman Pat.

Classic adult fiction also features red haired characters;

The Prisoner of Zenda by Anthony Hope Hawkins, the novel is about Rudolf Rossendyll who has a red head in every generation of the family.

Sherlock Holmes mystery The Red Headed League features a society of redheads.

Robert A. Heinlein cult science fiction writer features redheads many of his stories and was proud of his love of redheads.

Monachrome redheads

Many stars of the black and white film era were red heads, obviously film goers were often unaware of actors true hair colour. There continues to be far more red haired actresses than actors.

* Clara Bow
– The first red headed film star, she is also credited for bringing sex to the silverscreen, and was the first actress to flaunt her sex appeal.

* James Cagney
– He is best known for playing gangsters but also appeared in musicals, he had the nickname 'Red'.

* Greer Garson

– Born in London she became a Hollywood star. Greer received a record five consecutive Oscar nominations and also has the record for the longest acceptance speech

* Bette Davis

– The first actress to receive ten Academy Award nominations and the first woman to receive a Lifetime Achievement Award from the American Film Institute.

* Katherine Hepburn

– She holds the record for the most Best Actress Oscar's with a tally of four. In 1999 the American Film Institute named her the top film star of all time

* Stan Laurel

– Born in Ulverston, Cumbria, he spent his early years performing in musical hall across northern England, Stan went to Hollywood to become a global star.

When Laurel and Hardy films black and white films were colorised, he was inaccurately given brown hair.

* Spencer Tracey

– Made the top ten in the American Film Institutes 1999 list of greatest males stars of all time, romantically linked to Katherine Hepburn both on and off–screen.

"My husband said he wanted to have a relationship with a redhead, so I died my hair."

Jane Fonda

People who have died their hair red

* Cilla Black

* David Bowie

* Jo Brand

* Kathy Burke

* Tanni Grey–Thompson

* Annie Lenox

* Davina McCall

* Britney Spears

* Ruby Wax

Music

Italian composer and virtuoso violinist Vivaldi is without question the most famous classical composer with red hair, he was nicknamed "The Red Priest" (Il Prete Rosso).

Pop music has numerous redheaded musicians across a wide range of genres, the following is a list of singers;

Tori Amos, Belinda Carlisle, Carol Decker, Kiki Dee, Art Garfunkel, Noddy Holder, Mick Hucknall, Lulu (not sure if she is natural), Kirsty MacColl, Loreena McKennitt, Van Morrison, Willie Nelson, Harry Nilsson, Bonnie Rait, Eddi

Reader, Craig and Charley Reid (The Proclaimers), Axl Rose and Sonia to name a few of the most famous.

Sport

Throughout sporting history redheads have achieved top accolades, considering such a small percentage of the population have red hair it is amazing that there are so many top redheaded sports stars.

Boris Becker

German tennis star Boris Becker is the youngest player to win Wimbledon at the age of 17 and a six times Grand Slam singles champion.

Christopher Chattaway

Chris Chattaway took part in the race to break the four minute mile and was the first BBC Sports Personality of the Year in 1954, the year that he broke the world 5000m record. After athletics he went on to become a government minister. In 1995 in was knighted.

Paul Collingwood

All round criketer from Co Durham. Paul Collingwood has captained England and was a member of the team that won the Ashes in 2005.

Steve Davis

Steve Davis won the snooker world champoinship six times and dominated the sport thoughout the 1980s.

Rod Laver

Australian tennis star, Rod Laver was worlds top player for seven consecutive years. He is the only player in history to win all four Grand Slam singles titles in the same year. Rod Laver is considered by a number of expeerts to be the greatest tennis player in the history of the game.

Jack Nicklaus

Widely regarded to be the greatest golfer of all time. Jack Nicklaus won a record eighteen professional majors on the PGA Tour. His nickname is "The Golden Bear."

Alan Ball

Considered by many to be greatest ginger haired footballer. Alan Ball was the youngest player in the 1966 world cup squad and won the man of the match award for his perfomance in the final. He died in 2007.

Steve McClaren

Steve McClaren is the current manager of England, his previous job was managing Middlesbrough where he led them to victory in the 2004 Carling Cup and the team's first trophy.

In February 2001 BBC Sport Online named their 'Ginger XI' football team.

Mark Beeny

Richard Gough

Alex McLeish

Gordon Strachan

Gordon McQueen

Nicky Butt

Stuart McCall

Neil Lennon

Paul Scholes

Alan Ball

John Hartson

Beijing taxi drivers have been forbidden to dye their hair red.

People named red or ginger

Whether we like it or not, people with red or ginger hair get nicknamed in recognition of our hair.

Red Adair

Possibly the world's most famous fireman, Red Adair was portrayed by John Wayne in the film Hellfighters.

Woody Allen

Respected film director, actor, comedian and jazz fan, Woody Allen was nicknamed 'Red'.

Ginger Baker

Influential and superstar drummer, Ginger Baker played in Britain's first supergroup, Cream with Eric Clapton.

Red Ellen

Firebrand M.P Ellen Wilkinson helped organise the Jarrow March to London with a petition to campaign for jobs during the great recession.

Red Garland

Jazz pianist, Red Garland played in the Miles Davis Quintet in the late 1950s.

Ginger McCain

National Hunt trainer, Ginger McCain trained the three times Grand National Winner Red Rum (1973, 1974, 1977) and the 2004 winner Amberleigh House.

Ginger Rogers

Ginger Rogers had a film career that spanned fifty years and over seventy films. Best known for her role as Fred Astair's romantic interest and dancing partner in a series of ten Hollywood musicals.

Red Rodney

Be-bop trumpeter who is best known for playing with Charlie Parker's quintet. The only white member of the group, he was billed as Albino Red when playing in southern U.S.A.

"Once in his life, every man is entitled to fall madly in love with a gorgeous redhead."

Lucille Ball

Redhaired Beauties

Generations of the world's most acclaimed, talented, charasmatic actresses are redheads. Hollywood clearly appreciates the beauty of red hair.

Gillian Anderson

Voted "Sexist Woman in the World" by discerning lads mag FHM. Gillian Anderson is best known for playing Dana Scully in the X Files.

Rita Hayworth

In the 1940s Rita Hayworth was the decade's number one sex symbol and American forces favourite. Hayworth was one of the first Hispanic–Americans actresses to get leading roles in Hollywood.

Deborah Kerr

Scottish born Deborah Kerr played a number of romantic Hollywood roles. In from 'Here to Eternity' there is an iconic scene when she makes love to Burt Lancaster on a beach as waves crash over them.

Nicole Kidman

In 2006 Nicole Kidman was the highest paid actress in the film industry. Kidman has dual Australian and USA citizenship, she is also a Goodwill Ambassador for UNICEF.

Marilyn Monroe

Born Norma Jean Morteson and a redhead, sadly she decided to become a blond. One of the 20th centuries top sex symbols and box office draws, her image is iconic.

Maureen O'Hara

Born in Dublin, discovered by Charles Laughton she went on to star in many films with John Wayne and others. Maureen O'Hara was once considered to be one of the most beautiful woman in the world.

Molly Ringwald

A teenager in the 1980s, Molly Ringwald was Hollywood's top teenage actress and ranked number 1 in VH1's list of '100 Greatest Teen Stars"

Julia Roberts

Julia Roberts has been included in People magazines "50 Most Beautiful People in the World" eleven times and was the world's highest paid actress for four consecutive years.

Susan Sarandon

Susan Sarandon played Janet in the Rocky Horror Picture Show, the longest running theatrical release in history. A top box office star for four decades and human rights campaigner.

Tommy Clarkson

Tommy Clarkson is one of the greatest men in British history. A leading campaigner against the slave trade. William Wilberforce may get most of the credit for the abolition of slavery, but redhead Tommy Clarkson was the foremost abolitionist.

Galileo

Galileo has been given the accolades of the father of modern science and the father of modern physics.

Perhaps best known as an astronomer, his discoveries benefited by Galileo's developments in telescope design.

Websites

There are an increasing number of websites, the following have been a great resource in researching information for this book;

Gingernation.com
Hairweb.org
Purgatory.net
Realmofredheads.com
Redandproud.com

Gatherings

Massive gatherings of redheads take place each year in the Netherlands (the first meeting was in 2005, followed by 2007 and one is scheduled for 2008).

The meetings are mainly attended by woman and attract people from accross the world.

Society

In France there has been so much hostility to red heads that a society has been formed; Association Francoise des Rousses. Red hair is particularly rare in France with 0.03% of the population.

Eric the Red

Eric the Red is a character in an Icelandic saga about Nordic men discovering Canada and North America, set around the time of the first millenium.

Statistics

The U.K has the greatest concentration of redheads, with in places up to 13% of the population having red hair and possibly as many as 40% with the gene.

The further north you travel, the more redheads you

will find and when you reach Scotland you will see redheads everywhere.

Ireland has the second highest concentration of redheads, with approximately 10% of the population.

The United States has the largest population of redheads, but estimates of the percentage of the population range from only 2% to 6%.

On a global basis red hair is a physical feature that is mainly found in Europe, all though in history it is recorded in north Africa and Asia. In the 21st century red hair is considered to be a sign of celtic roots.

Ginger Whinger

A derrogatory term given to people who point out that it is tiresome and unpleasant to bully and tease people with red hair.

Perhaps the most famous ginger whinger is Chris Evans who has highlighted the problems suffered by many children.

Gingerism

A term that has been coined to describe the negative treatment of redhaired people.

Sadly, it is often used sarcastically. Discrimination against people with red hair is not a problem on the same scale as other discrimination, however, it is still unacceptable.

Redheads
stand out in
a crowd, and
are more easily
remembered
than people
with common
hair colours.